C000200347

# WILLIAM YEOWARD
## at home

# WILLIAM YEOWARD
## at home
### elegant living in town and country

photography by **GAVIN KINGCOME**

**CICO BOOKS**
LONDON NEW YORK

*This book without question is for Colin*

This edition published in 2015 by CICO Books
an imprint of Ryland Peters & Small
341 E 116th St, New York NY 10029
20–21 Jockey's Fields, London WC1R 4BW
www.rylandpeters.com

First published in 2010 by CICO Books

10 9 8 7 6 5 4 3

Text © CICO Books 2010
Design and photography © CICO Books 2010

The author's moral rights have been asserted. All rights reserved.
No part of this publication may be reproduced, stored in a
retrieval system, or transmitted in any form or by any means,
electronic, mechanical, photocopying, or otherwise, without the
prior permission of the publisher.

A CIP catalog record for this book is available from the Library
of Congress and the British Library.

ISBN: 978 1 78249 237 5

Printed in China

Design: Christine Wood
Photography: Gavin Kingcome
Illustration on endpapers: Roger Hall

# CONTENTS

# INTRODUCTION

I don't see myself as either a town person or a country person – but as both. So I count myself extremely fortunate in having two homes, one in that glorious region of England, the Cotswolds, and the other in the heart of London. They couldn't be more different but each 'satisfies a need'.

I love my house in the country for all sorts of reasons. It has a sentimental attachment because my great aunt lived in it for a time, but if I'm really honest, the reason I bought it probably has as much, if not more, to do with the fact that I'm a very visual person. I am always drawn to houses that are quirky and pleasing to look at, and my house, with its pointed gothic windows, quatrefoils and crisply carved stonework, is a joy.

It's no exaggeration to say that, when I took it on 18 years ago, it was dreadful in every way. It was tatty and the layout just didn't 'work'. But I could see it had potential and, although not large overall, it gave scope for a wonderful, big drawing room, perfect for quenching my passion for entertaining.

Just across the garden is a small cottage, which I bought a few years ago to convert for guests. This has proved a huge success, as my friends come to us for meals, or just to chat, but they sleep in the cottage, where there is also a sitting room, so they can be independent and quiet if they wish.

Deep down, I think of my country house as 'home', but my work is mainly in London and there is no denying that I enjoy the stimulation of urban life during the week. I have an apartment in a 1900s block, which has a good, solid feel to it, and

LEFT: *This sums up the atmosphere in my drawing room in the country: it's all about comfort, but, with its mix of fabrics and patterns, it has elements of surprise, which I consider essential.*

I have decorated it in a manner that is slightly 'sharper' than in my home in the country – though not, of course, at the expense of comfort!

I share both the apartment in London and the house in Gloucestershire with Colin Orchard, who is an interior designer. Colin has had what I call a 'proper' training and background in design, and he has a terrific eye for proportion and colour. We both have strong views about decoration but he tempers any of my wayward instincts with a more classical approach, and somehow we manage to agree.

This is my third book, and it is the most personal. Focusing on what pleases one's own aesthetic preferences is something that comes from one's very core. I could not be more grateful to have chosen as my life's work the creation of beautiful pieces for interiors, and I am blessed to have two very different laboratories in which to test and hone my skills. My country house has a magical karma and personality that have a great affect on all who visit, and, in London, I live in an apartment that fits me like a glove. In these two places, I am able to experiment, improve and judge the effect of my work and, together with Colin, enjoy the style that we have jointly created.

*William Yeoward*

RIGHT: *Here is my drawing room in London. In contrast to my home in the country, it has a 'sharper', more contemporary ambience and is furnished with pieces that are more idiosyncratic.*

# COUNTRY ROOMS
## FOR LIVING

ABOVE: *In the 'new' porch, I have left exposed the stonework that was formerly part of the exterior wall of the schoolmistress's cottage. I like the ruggedness – it seems appropriate in a transitional space between inside and outside.*

LEFT: *Walking sticks in a handsome container look decorative, so I have placed them in full view right by the door.*

RIGHT: *The metal gates, entrance door and flanking windows are a panoply of gothic. I wanted them to reflect the architecture of the house.*

BELOW: *An antiques-dealer friend found this wooden crate in a flea market and couldn't resist giving it to me – spot the name!*

PREVIOUS PAGES: *The area in front of the old school-house, which faces the lane, is gravelled for cars. I haven't gone in for flowers here – just evergreens clipped to form strong, simple shapes, and I've planted some of them in big, zinc buckets.*

# THE PORCH AND ENTRANCE

My house was originally two separate buildings – a Victorian school-house and, a few feet away, the schoolmistress's cottage – which, after conversion, were linked together in the 1970s. By the time I arrived 18 years ago, everything was looking horrendously tatty, but the more fundamental challenge was that the layout was completely hopeless for the way we wanted to live. I came to the conclusion that the only solution was to tear down the entire link and start again, reconfiguring the space to create a new entrance, complete with the porch shown here, and hall. I retained the porch on the schoolhouse – seen in the previous pages – and the one on the cottage, as they are an integral part of the original architecture, but they are no longer used.

# THE HALL

Halls should be welcoming but you have to think about practicalities, too, so here I've used wooden flooring and patterned rugs rather than plain carpet. To get as much natural light as possible into the interior, which occupies the gap between the two original buildings, I introduced an elegant version of a skylight – a large, rectangular lantern. I also used gothic cornice to continue the style of the external architecture.

RIGHT: *Halls generally look best when furnished simply and boldly. The marble-topped table is a perfect stage for a group of objects with different shapes and textures. The large picture above is framed minimally to complement the simple look.*

BELOW: *Architectural stone fragments contrast with the wooden clock case and leafy plants.*

The hall is a continuous space from the new entrance porch to the stairs, but there is a change in flooring: wooden boards in the newly built part and stone in the old part. The walls throughout are painted in a stony yellow. Yellow isn't always the easiest colour, as it can be too 'warm' or too 'thin', but this shade, which is reminiscent of Bath stone, works well and is a good backdrop for pictures and – my favourite – blue-and-white ceramics. All the woodwork is painted white, except the new staircase, which is made of English oak and was inspired by the servants' staircase in a grand house in Devon of the same date as my more modest home.

LEFT: *This part of the hall has a rather Continental countenance, probably because the clock is Scandinavian, the table Portuguese and the chair Italian – and all are painted. At the far end is a symmetrical arrangement using jars: the large one beneath the table helps to fill the gap between the legs, a space which can often look unpleasantly empty in a setting such as here, where you look directly at it.*

RIGHT: *This view shows the mix of materials in the hall: stone, iron, terracotta and oak. They have a natural affinity.*

LEFT: *The door from the hall to the back yard has gothic detailing. A nineteenth-century Italian terracotta figure of a Sienese merchant cuts a dash alongside a boarded recess filled with ceramics. They aren't there purely for appearance – I use them, too.*

ABOVE: *On the wall behind the door is an engraved portrait of a gentleman within an oval cartouche. I topped the frame with a carving of Prince of Wales feathers – they add a bit of interest and look jaunty.*

OVERLEAF: *There's so much to appreciate in the patterns on these ceramics that you need to take a close look: freely drawn flowers, a sentimental couple and a ship approaching a port. The animals are charming for being so naïve.*

# THE CLOAKROOM

As anyone who lives in the country will tell you, a designated room for coats, boots, hats, rackets and all the rest of the paraphernalia that goes with the territory is a godsend. Our cloakroom is in the most practical position of all in the house, being directly inside the back door, and, equally practically, it has a stone floor. If you have just come in from tramping across muddy fields or bashing a ball about a dusty tennis court, a hard-wearing surface, such as Cotswold stone, is essential. You also need somewhere to sit when you take off your boots or plimsolls, and I have the perfect thing: a triple bench that was made around 1900 for the shoe department of a store in the north of England. It has come full circle in serving a similar purpose here.

There seems to be more 'weather' in the country, or at least we are more conscious of it, and we need the 'kit' to cope with it, fair or foul. I find hats very amusing, and although most of those in my cloakroom are genuinely used to keep off the sun or rain, I own up to having others that are there just because they give me so much pleasure to look. Old velvet caps, especially those with embroidery, are minor works of art.

LEFT: *The midnight blue of the velvet and the silver embroidery are too beautiful for this cap to be hidden away.*

RIGHT: *The recess was created not only for coats but also with an eye to the future: hidden in the projections to either side are all the services we would need if we ever wanted to install a bathroom on the ground floor. Wide, horizontal planking conceals the pipework-in-waiting.*

## THE DRAWING ROOM

The drawing room occupies one of the Victorian schoolrooms which was used by the juniors. It has wonderful volume, thanks to the high ceiling, and it's big enough to take lots of chairs and a capacious sofa, which makes it a brilliant space for entertaining. It's where our parties usually start and end. I find that rooms where everything matches run the risk of looking staid, which is a dampener at any time but particularly for a party. You need to mix things up, introduce contrast, take a few chances – that way the interior becomes much more interesting and stimulating. Here, I chose blue for the walls, then I added colours, mainly limey greens and burnt oranges, that aren't the most obvious partners for blue but, to me, they bring the whole thing to life. In fact, I'm not happy with a scheme unless there's a bit of 'clash'!

The windows are spectacular, so I didn't want to hide them, but I felt they needed curtains, especially in winter. The question was: what sort? Plain curtains would look sad in the context, so I opted for a scheme that, although fairly elaborate, does not hide the window arch. It acts as a frame and, during the day at least, allows the architecture to be appreciated.

ABOVE: *Clear, cut crystal provides a quiet counterbalance in rooms where there are lots of objects – it's 'there but not there'. These table centrepieces and covered dishes have beautiful shapes and reflective qualities. My fascination with crystal objects is involved with forms and scale as much as material and faceting.*

LEFT: *The furniture is centred on the fireplace and underpinned by a large, colourful, oriental rug. The outline of the eighteenth-century Italian mirror creates interestingly shaped spaces to either side, which allow for objects of different heights to be placed on the chimneypiece. The tall candelabra spring from urn bases and are hung with glass drops; the modern, papier-mâché figures are by Jane Strawbridge.*

LEFT: *The arrangement with seed heads is skeletal and the vase transparent, so neither interferes too much with the view through the window. The lacquer table is partnered by a lacquer-and-gilt Regency chair and a wing chair upholstered in velvet with a pattern that echoes the organic elements in the room.*

RIGHT: *When an opening was introduced to link the drawing room with the new hall, the arch was designed to overcome the visual disparity between the lofty ceiling height in the former and the lower height in the latter. The double doors have pointed, gothic-motif panels in keeping with the architectural style of the room. The Scandinavian clock has an anthropomorphic form that always makes me smile.*

PREVIOUS PAGES: *When the room was a schoolroom, the sills were higher, presumably to prevent the children from gazing through the windows when they should have been paying attention to their mistress. I lowered the sills to bring in more light — and enable me to look out. How different! The curtain treatment, with its swagged and tailed pelmets, is Colin's interpretation of a John Fowler design. Lighting is provided by table lamps, small floor lamps and a 1960s papier-mâché chandelier. Above the sofa is a handsome, embroidered hatchment.*

LEFT: *At one end of the drawing room is a 'Cherington' glazed cabinet. Like much of my William Yeoward Collection of furniture, it is inspired by a traditional design but given a tweak — for example, an interesting paint finish — so that it doesn't look 'repro'. The curtains are made of embroidered, patterned silk, edged with plain green silk velvet, and both fabrics are used for the fringed pelmet. Resting on the sill, and seemingly enjoying the sunshine, is a ceramic lion; his partner is on another sill in the room. Although we have a separate library, there is never enough space in our house for books, so we pile them up on tables in other rooms, as you can see here. (I always feel a bit wary of houses where there are no books!)*

RIGHT: *The objects in my house tend to be fairly random in style and have been bought, often on impulse, for no other reason than I like them — which, of course, is the best reason of all. On one of the tables next to the sofa is a group that makes the point: a terracotta pot decorated with bacchanalian themes, some family photographs, a covered candle, a strange animal and a pretty lustre dish.*

## THE LIBRARY

Our library is a relaxed alternative to the drawing room. It's the place where we and our weekend guests tend to congregate for reading the papers on Sunday mornings or for whiling away the day if the weather doesn't tempt us outside. It's designed to be leisurely and sociable, with plenty of chairs: soft for those who like to nestle near the fireplace, and upright for others who want to sit at the Arts-and-Crafts table by the bookcase at the opposite end of the room. The walls are painted in a shade of green that has 'life' but is sympathetic to the paintings. Unlike in the drawing room, the library ceiling is not soaringly high, so a simpler curtain treatment was called for. Instead of a pelmet, I decided on a pole at cornice height and hung from it curtains with an uncomplicated heading. The fabric, one of my own designs, is a rough, printed linen, which I've edged with red velvet – I enjoy juxtaposing contrasting textures in this way. You see a similar red in the cushion on the armchair by the window and it reappears on the arms and for the piping on the striped wing chair. I like piping, as it gives definition to upholstery, so I've also used it on the sofa.

LEFT: *The stone chimneypiece is a straightforward bolection design with a fairly shallow projection, which limits the size of the things we can put on the top of it. The pictures depict a curious mix of subjects, including a group of men in a working men's club in north-east England, painted in the mid-twentieth century by Adrian Hill. This down-to-earth picture dominates the wall above the sofa, while the colourful one on the fireplace wall portrays characters from a fairground.*

ABOVE: *A whole wall of books can look oppressive and ponderous, but interspersing a few decorative objects immediately lightens the effect.*

LEFT: *Although the specially commissioned bookcase fills virtually the entire end wall of the library, it is freestanding rather than 'fitted'. You have to be careful about introducing ceiling-high, wall-to-wall 'fitted' furniture to a room, especially in an old house, as it can change the proportions of the interior and give it a totally different (and usually less satisfactory) feeling. In this room, for instance, the space between the window and far wall is quite narrow. If the bookcase had been built to the full height of the room and extended across the full width, it would not only have jammed right up against the window architrave — not attractive! — but also made the room seem shorter.*

LEFT: *This commanding figure on a window sill has turned his back on the outside world.*

BELOW LEFT: *There is never a day when the house is without flowers. I use whatever varieties happen to be available and enjoy seeing how I can make them live together happily.*

BELOW: *Cushions and throws contribute to the library's cosy atmosphere. I often move the cushions around as it's an easy way to effect small changes to a room and encourage you to see things afresh. Sometimes this chair has the cushion shown here; at other times, it could be a bright red one, or a striped one.*

RIGHT: *The sofa is covered in an 'old' shade of aubergine. Piping, in a paler, coordinating colour, outlines the whole thing, including the seat cushions, and is picked up by a narrow band of the same fabric along the bottom edge of the skirt. The x-frame stool in the foreground offers an additional 'perch' for sitting when it isn't spread with books.*

LEFT: *When you enter a dining room, the first things you see are usually the backs of chairs, which can look dull. Using contrasting fabrics overcomes this – and the fabric on the backs needn't be upholstery quality.*

BELOW: *Part of my embarrassingly large and ever-growing collection of decanters!*

BELOW RIGHT: *The damson colour of the flowers has an uplifting vibrancy.*

## THE DINING ROOM

The difficulty with dining rooms is not so much how to dress them up for entertaining as how to ensure that they don't have a forlorn, forgotten air when they are not being used – which, of course, is nine-tenths of the time. I like to leave my dining-room door open and I make sure the room affords attractive glimpses when I pass by – the upholstery fabric on the chairs is colourful and there are always flowers on the table, so I never feel this is a shut-off, wasted space.

RIGHT: *When I entertain, I want my friends to be comfortable – hence the deep-buttoned seats and backs to the chairs. (Incidentally, I notice that when guests are seated on chairs that are almost as comfortable as beds, they tend to linger longer and the consumption of claret goes up!) The chairs at either end of the ebony-inlaid table are different but continue the buttoned theme. I am no respecter of putting together things of the same period: the papier-mâché sconces are modern, the French pearwood commode dates from the 1820s, the velvet-covered chairs are my versions of Regency and the 'end' chairs are 1940s-inspired… and so it goes on.*

BELOW: *I rarely like sets of matching dining chairs – I prefer variety, so long as it is visually pleasing. Here, the buttons link the various colours of the upholstery.*

# THE KITCHEN

The original schoolhouse comprised two rooms – one for juniors, the other for infants – linked by double doors. My drawing room now occupies the junior room, while my kitchen, which is the pulse of the house, takes up the infants' space. Both rooms have similarly tall, arched windows and high ceilings but the overall proportions of the interiors feel very different. The kitchen seems much more vertical and cries out for interest at high level to make the room hold together visually. When we're entertaining more formally, I like to get in professional help, so I planned the kitchen and dining room to be adjacent to one another but separated by a short corridor, allowing the 'help' to be nearby but get on with things unseen from the dining room. A pantry opens off the corridor.

LEFT: *The Aga spans most of the wall between the door to the hall (at left) and the passage (at right) to the pantry and dining room. Above the Aga is a shelf displaying apothecary jars; higher still, providing all-important scale and interest in the upper reaches of the room, a nineteenth-century Dutch portrait of a woman filleting fish is partnered by coats of arms. I love the idea of having a stone floor in a kitchen but it can be very clattery in a room where a lot of walking-about goes on, and the sound of chairs being scraped across it is horrendous, so I've used a quieter finish – proper, old-fashioned linoleum tiles, laid diagonally, in a traditional chequer pattern.*

RIGHT AND OVERLEAF: *The dresser, with shelves and back panel painted to correspond with the colour of the walls, is sited where double doors used to separate the infants' and juniors' schoolrooms. It's a blown-up version of what people dream about for a country kitchen. A window seat, piled with cushions, is a comfortable spot for friends to sit while I am cooking. The fine-quality, 1840s armorial chairs are made of oak, as is the table. The latter is scrubbed rather than polished: if you have a polished-wood table in your kitchen, you just make work for yourself.*

## THE PANTRY

The pantry opens off the short passage between the kitchen and dining room and is glimpsed here through the glazed door. Although some provisions are kept in the pantry, my real joy is the vintage kitchenalia it houses, which I arrange with as much pride as if it were the most priceless Sèvres. The shapes of these wares are unselfconsciously beautiful, and I am often struck by how frequently these forms appear in other guises – in old crystal bowls, for instance. It's as though those early makers had found, from generations of experience, what they considered to be the ideal shapes for the purposes, and they didn't feel compelled to change them. Nowadays, we are always trying to be 'different'. Perhaps we could learn a lesson or two from these early pieces.

LEFT: *Seen from the kitchen, the pantry is at left. The baskets in the lower part of the room are for table linens – checks, spots, stripes and, of course, plain.*

RIGHT: *I am completely lacking in discipline when it comes to buying vintage kitchenalia of this kind. The monochrome tones look wonderful on the pantry's slate shelves as well as on the white-painted ones above.*

OVERLEAF: *Old French carafes and Hungarian plates… these are nothing more than 'peasantware' pieces but I delight in their honest beauty and integrity.*

# THE LANDING

Architecturally, there is nothing intrinsically special about this space, so it was a matter of making the most of it by adding some interesting decorative details. A detail that has worked really well can be seen on the tray ceiling. Previously, this was a plain, blank expanse that met the walls abruptly, without a cornice. In fact, we wouldn't have wanted a cornice in the conventional sense, as it would have looked too pretentious here, but we did see a need for something to soften the meeting point. Well, it's surprising what you can do with lengths of broom handle! We ran this round the top of the walls, and from corner to corner across the ceiling, then painted it white to tie the whole thing together. This has imbued the space with interest without looking showy.

Another problem we faced on the landing was the deep, rather low opening into my bedroom. Any structural change here would have been too disruptive, so I decided on a much simpler solution, which was to treat the wall space above the opening as a sort of 'over-door' and hang it with a gilded carving. I don't know the provenance of the carving but I suspect it once formed part of an elaborate bed.

LEFT: *There are two bedrooms opening off the landing, each with its own bathroom. The window overlooks the lantern in the roof of the hall below.*

TOP RIGHT: *A contemporary chandelier by Farfelus Farfadets is the centrepiece of the landing. It is made of papier mâché, which gives softer edges than metal and, with its gilded finish, has echoes of those splendid, antique carvings one sees in Venice and Florence.*

RIGHT: *The balusters on the staircase and landing combine two different designs but are evenly spaced where they meet the floor and handrail.*

## MY BEDROOM

The schoolmistress's cottage was originally a two-up, two-down building, with a small lean-to kitchen. We converted the two downstairs rooms into the library and the two upstairs ones into my bedroom. (It didn't take much to knock through the dividing walls, as they were paper-thin.) The inspiration for the decoration of the bedroom followed a visit to Endsleigh in Devon, a hotel where Olga Polizzi has created very stylish decoration schemes within a picturesque, early-nineteenth-century *cottage ornée*. One of the schemes I particularly admired had a design painted on the walls. The large scale of the pattern slightly altered, in the nicest way, the visual proportions of the room and made me feel I was in a doll's house: it was grandeur in miniature. The exotic wallpaper in my own bedroom is even more over-scaled, and it's bolder, a veritable jungle of orange flowers. When there is as much pattern as this defining the space, you can't put too many more patterns into the mix — hence the plain curtains.

LEFT: *The expanse of wall between the two windows looked disproportionately long and blank so we added a chimney-piece. An armchair and table provide a comfortable place for reading.*

BELOW: *Books and a lamp for reading, plus a Portuguese farmer (in fact, a ceramic whistle!) for company.*

BELOW RIGHT: *A portrait of an Irish peer attired in Indian fancy dress hangs above the Continental chest.*

OVERLEAF: *The curtains are plain cotton ottoman edged with linen, a placid foil for the vibrant patterns.*

## MY BATHROOM

The bathroom leads directly off the bedroom but, with a sloping ceiling coming down to the exterior wall, it has a different architectural character, which called for a more restrained, even cottagey, style of decoration. The deep window reveal ruled out curtains but a blind with a large print makes a connection with the patterned walls of the bedroom. In front of the window is a really pretty, early-nineteenth-century table with a painted finish, and on it are two aloes in terracotta flowerpots. I buy new flowerpots by the pallet-load and leave them outdoors until they have lost their youth and look mature enough to be allowed inside. The ceiling by the basin is very low, but an articulated French shaving mirror fits the space and is practical.

LEFT: *The bathroom walls are painted in a subtle shade I can only dub 'greige'. The picture at top right depicts Barbara Hepworth's garden and is by Cornish artist Colin Orchard – no relation to the Colin Orchard of this book! In fact, it wasn't until after we had decided to buy the picture that we realised the coincidence of the name.*

RIGHT: *Aloes thrive in the light by the window. Like cacti, these plants are underrated for use indoors, where they can add a strong, sculpture element. The bath panel is classically fluted.*

# THE BLUE ROOM

Blue and chocolate is without doubt one of my favourite palettes and I have indulged my passion for it to the limit in this room – where, incidentally, there is a sloping ceiling. I point out the ceiling because it accounts for the top-right corner of the wardrobe being nicked off. The wardrobe was designed by me a while ago and has been moved several times during its existence but the finial was just too high for its latest (appropriately gothic) home. I don't think the loss of the finial matters; if anything, it enhances the charm.

LEFT: *The cloth is a nineteenth-century patchwork bedcover. I didn't have a place for it when I bought it ten years ago but now it has come into its own, which is very satisfying.*

BELOW: *Putting together different textures can create an effect that is way beyond the sum of the parts.*

The wall height below the sloping ceiling in the 'blue room' is low, which led to several problems – apart from how to accommodate the tall, gothic wardrobe opposite the bed. One of the conundrums was devising a bedhead. If it were low, it would have appeared mean and still wouldn't have left enough space above it to hang a picture or other decorative embellishment. We could have opted for a *lit à la polonaise*, which would have gone up into the pitch, but we felt that would be overpowering. So, instead, we came up with a bedhead in a tall, round-headed design upholstered with a wide stripe, which introduces an element of verticality – as does the pair of large lamps to either side of the bed. There are numerous fabrics in the room: the one used for the blind was a chance buy of a five-metre length of hand-embroidered silk, which became the starting point for the entire scheme. Through a door to the left of the painted table with candle slides is a shower room.

ABOVE LEFT: *Vintage cotton towels are worth looking out for as they have such appealing patterns, textures and colours. These ones weren't bought specifically for the 'blue room' bathroom but, serendipitously, have found a place here.*

LEFT: *In this view, which looks across the end of the bed and the bench at its foot, you can see the shower room framed by the door architrave. The shower itself, at left, is generously proportioned and lined with natural-stone mosaic, which serves the purpose beautifully.*

RIGHT: *Here is a northern European 'moment': above an eighteenth-century Scandinavian table, which retains its original paint finish and has candle slides that pull out from beneath the faux-marble top, is a late-eighteenth-century Scandinavian portrait, painted in watercolour. The handsome pot was made in Stoke on Trent, probably in the 1840s.*

PREVIOUS PAGES: *The room has been given an element of verticality with a tall bedhead and, to either side, a pair of impressively large, crystal lamps from my Collection. They are made by a technique similar to that used in the days of ancient Rome, but the threads of molten glass drizzled over the surface have been 'super-volumed' for a modern look. The chest of drawers, with rope edging and drop handles, is an English Arts and Crafts piece.*

THE GUEST COTTAGE

RIGHT: *Flanking the door to the cottage are Northern European olive trees in tubs. The formality of the arrangement lends distinction to the plain entrance.*

LEFT *The detailing of the back of the front door was adapted from a gate I saw in New England. I suppose you could describe the entire scheme in this part of the cottage as 'New England comes to the Cotswolds'. There is a freshness about it, yet I feel sure the blue-grey colour of the paint is an 'old' colour: it has warmth and isn't aggressive.*

PREVIOUS PAGES: *An old well head encloses a 'ball' water feature along the path from the main house to the cottage, which you can see in the distance. The obelisks are copies of nineteenth-century Virginian dovecotes.*

## THE COTTAGE ENTRANCE

The guest cottage is reached from the main house along a gravel path and through a pair of iron gates. It's only a short walk but it is enough to give guests a sense of independence and for none of us to feel that we are living on top of one another. Compared with the heart-stoppingly pretty exterior of the main house, with its finely carved gothic detailing, the exterior of the guest cottage, built in the 1960s, is a Plain Jane. When we took the building on, we decided against doing anything too ambitious to the outside but simply to paint the stucco a warm shade of ochre, then add some style by the use of symmetry. This simple, geometric device can work wonders in unpromising situations! The small, front garden is bisected by a paved path, with low planting outlining the grass; the entrance door is flanked by trees in tubs made of cast iron with timber linings; and, piling symmetry on symmetry, the trees are in turn flanked by huge stone balls. We did, however, do a massive amount of work to the interior of the cottage. In fact, we completely gutted it, but the one thing we couldn't alter was the position of the entrance. As a result, and it has proved to be a happy outcome, the wall opposite the front door has been constructed on a curve. This was done to allow for the sweep of the door and to give comfortable space for circulation.

# THE COTTAGE SITTING ROOM

The sitting room is open to the hall but has a feeling of separation, thanks to the stairs, which are sited between the two spaces. As the staircase is so prominent, it was imperative that it should look interesting but, equally importantly, it had to be in keeping with the modest setting. We have used simple, square-section spindles of the kind you find in cottages all over Britain but, more unusually, they are grouped in threes on the treads. I think the design is a success, and I am especially pleased with the newel post, which is an inverted replica of the stepped plinth of the chimneypiece. This detail is a kind of homage to that masterful decorator, the late Roger Banks-Pye, who was a friend and devised the chimneypiece.

LEFT: *The Italian, cut velvet used for the curtains must be the most expensive fabric I have ever bought, and I refuse to give it up! It is now in its third incarnation. Behind the early-twentieth-century, wooden loggia table is an old trumpet banner. The woven stripe on the chair reminds me of a horse blanket and is from my Collection.*

RIGHT: *The cushions on the sofa are made up from antique textiles.*

OVERLEAF: *Just about all the internal features in the guest cottage are new. We ran beams across the ceiling purely to give it some texture. The room is quite low and, without some sort of definition overhead, the space could have seemed shoe-boxy.*

# THE COTTAGE BEDROOMS AND BATHROOMS

*LEFT: There is nothing wrong with having a beautiful room in the old-fashioned sense, and this is what I aimed at in my parents' bedroom. The curtains are an old toile that I have kept for years. I can never bear to throw away lovely textiles and, eventually, they always find a new role.*

*BELOW: A chest fits snugly between the room's two curved walls.*

*BELOW RIGHT: Guest bedrooms need flowers and plants to ensure they feel lived-in rather than only used occasionally.*

One of the bedrooms in the cottage – the one seen here – was designed especially for my adored parents. I wanted it to have a rather nostalgic feel, with old-fashioned comforts, whereas the other bedroom, though also very comfortable, has a slightly younger, more contemporary edge to it. Both rooms have their own bathroom, which is en suite – an arrangement that all guests appreciate and every host should strive to offer, even in the smallest house.

I'm not keen on rooms with odd shapes and always find myself wanting to regularize them. The curved wall just inside the entrance to the cottage forms one of the walls in my parents' bedroom. While I like the curve by the entrance, where the space is altogether more complicated, I couldn't bear the asymmetry it created in the bedroom, so I added another curve to balance it. Within this curve is a wardrobe. There is a short stretch of straight wall between the two arcs, which provides a perfect spot for a chest of drawers.

There were no such issues with the shape of the other bedroom in the cottage. It was just a matter of decorating and giving interest with well-chosen colours, textiles and furniture.

The walls above the dado in my parents' bedroom are painted in an elusive shade of pale violet, not too pink and not too blue. This truly lovely colour is offset by the soft white of the tongue-and-groove dado and the ceiling (which, like the sitting room, has painted beams). The door leading from the bedroom to the bathroom is part-glazed. I like using part-glazed doors, so long as the situation is right for them, as they look so much more interesting than solid ones. In this instance, where the room is intended for a couple, and where a walk-through dressing area comes between the bedroom and the bathroom, the need for a solid door is not imperative. The dressing area and bathroom are lined with tongue-and-groove boarding, giving continuity with the bedroom. My parents tell me that they are very comfortable in their 'suite', which is the best compliment I could receive. All designers like to think that they have achieved their objective and I am no exception to the rule!

LEFT: *The space between the bedroom and the bathroom is designed as a walk-through dressing area. On the walls are, at left, cartoons by Oliver Preston and, at right, a picture of our gothic house, by Liz Workman.*

RIGHT: *Between the pots is a cut-out made of reclaimed wood, painted by the late, talented fashion illustrator, Colin Barnes.*

PREVIOUS PAGES: *Two large, very grand English mirrors, dating from the eighteenth century, are handsome focal points in my parents' bedroom. The cushions to either side of the central one, which is made up with an antique, suzani panel, are by Sarah King, who designed many of the cushions throughout the house.*

*This is the guest cottage's second bedroom. The character is more lighthearted than in my parents' room but it is nevertheless a very comfortable place to be in. The room is not all that large, and it is conventional in shape, so I decided that the best way to furnish it would be symmetrically – in any case, I do like symmetry! To either side of the bed are tables from the English Arts and Crafts period with later, stone tops. Above them is a matched pair of 1950s mirrors, while the picture above the bed is a recent work by New Zealand artist Sarah Guppy. The juxtaposition of different periods creates interest. And at the foot of the bed? Well, a tuck box containing a few goodies is always welcome!*

As you can see on the previous pages and here, the second guest bedroom has a cheerful mix of styles and periods: for instance, laid across the end of the bed is a handsome piece of cutwork from India; facing the bed is an antique, Italian, painted chest; and then there is a mirror with a 'cut-out' frame, a design that is part of my William Yeoward Collection. Adjoining the bedroom is a bathroom lined with a Tricia Guild paper with the pattern highlighted in silver. Here, again, I have used one of my favourite types of door, with panes of glass in the upper half. It's a style I choose more for the visual interest than for the fact that the glazing

LEFT: *One of my 'cut-out' mirrors hangs above the Italian chest of drawers, which has ebonized columns and is positioned opposite the bed.*

BELOW: *On the chest is a series of tall, thin vessels in different colours. I love their etiolated forms, which look particularly good when grouped together.*

brings light from one room to another. On this particular door are a reclaimed ebony fingerplate, knob and escutcheon. There is a satisfying quality in these old pieces that is hard to replicate in new door furniture.

It's important that guest rooms don't have a sad, uninhabited ambience, so I furnish mine with just as many pictures and decorative objects as I have in my own bedroom. And I feel the same way about guest bathrooms: I use pictures, ceramics or whatever it takes to make the room feel loved and hospitable.

RIGHT: *Ranged along the bath surround, against the wall, are more vessels, though these are older and more purposeful than the elegant vessels in the bedroom. They are stoneware bottles for Normandy cider, probably made around 1860, which I love for their 'drab' colour.*

BELOW: *The vintage door furniture, made of ebony, is a delight. It enhances the door and feels wonderfully smooth to the touch. I have used the same style throughout the guest cottage, but for the schoolhouse I have collected pieces in many different designs and materials, and have placed them where I thought most appropriate.*

COUNTRY ENTERTAINING

## PARTY FLOWERS

Ideally, I get flowers from my own garden but sometimes there simply isn't anything out there, or perhaps I'm having the sort of celebration when exotic ones would 'tick the box' better than traditional English varieties. As you can see in the picture opposite, there are masses waiting in the porch of the old schoolhouse before being brought inside. I bought most of them at the market and chose them mainly for their bold shapes and unusual colours. The most important thing is not to be mean with flowers – and remember to buy them early, so that they have time to come out and be at their best when needed.

LEFT: *Since I reconfigured the link between the old schoolhouse and schoolmistress's cottage, the original schoolhouse entrance, seen here, is no longer used. However, the porch provides a cool, sheltered spot for storing flowers until I'm ready to sort and arrange them.*

RIGHT: *Putting together antique, dusty pink and strong blue is not immediately obvious but the combination can be very successful. Here, hyacinths are seen with roses in these two shades.*

PREVIOUS PAGES: *One advantage of having a big field in front of our house is that it affords a great deal more flexiblity for informal entertaining.*

## SUMMER LUNCH

Dining rooms are like chameleons – their appearance can be changed to suit different circumstances. When arranged for a summer lunch, my dining room has a totally different ambience from when it's set for dinner in winter. In summer, when the curtains are open and you can step straight into the garden through the French doors, it would look laboured for the table to be laden with huge amounts of tableware or smothered in dark, heavy colours. The impression has to be one of lightness, to match the season. 'Simple' is the key, but that doesn't mean that the china and glass have to be totally plain. Pale plates with pretty shapes and clear glasses with subtle detail provide interest whilst being unfussy. A few pebble vases of unpretentious flowers complete the delicate effect.

LEFT: *The only 'solid' colour on the table is seen in the napkins, which punctuate the summery freshness of the pale tableware arranged on a light cloth.*

RIGHT: The size and shape of the opening in a vase dictate the arrangement of the flowers just as much as the size and shape of the container itself. The pebble vases on my summer dining table are wide in comparison to their height, and the opening is narrow, so I can only fit in a few stems. The result reminds me of those lovely oriental flower prints, where maximum effect is achieved with minimum elements.

ABOVE: Lime green and pink is a stunning combination. I love the contrast between the papery quality of the peony petals and the filigree character of the Alchemilla mollis. If ever there were a combination that 'says' June in England, this is it.

RIGHT: The tablecloth and napkin fabrics are plain but have fairly robust textures, which gives them character. Old napkins with embroidered initials are so beautiful that I snap them up whenever I see them at antiques fairs and flea markets. It doesn't bother me that the letters don't match my name — they are part of the napkins' history and something to enjoy for their own sake. In the past, napkins like these were invariably white, but I sometimes have them dyed to give the table a more modern feel.

LEFT: *Most of the crystal on the table is clear, with cutting that refracts the summer light coming through the French doors. The water jug has a silver rim, which has subtle glamour and adds to the reflections.*

RIGHT: *There is no single, large flower arrangement on the table – instead, there are several vases dotted about in an informal manner, and they are low, enabling guests to talk across the table without visual interruption. (On dark evenings, if I put candlesticks on the table, I tend to have higher arrangements. These have to be placed much more precisely in order not to create any 'barriers'.) The lily painting is by Matthew Usmar Lauder.*

# WINTER DINNER

If you are as passionate about the tabletop as I am, a winter dinner party is the perfect excuse for getting out the Jag rather than the Ford. When I dress this room for summer parties, I keep the effect much simpler and 'cooler', but when the evenings are dark and the weather cold, I want a totally different effect, one that is full of warmth, glamour and 'stuff'. All too often people have cupboards crammed with beautiful things but leave them hidden away. I think that's a pity, especially at this time of year. Don't be shy: bring out the best china and crystal, reach for the silver, light the candles. And check what's at the back of the cupboards – you may find something you had forgotten about and that will add an element of surprise, which always makes a table interesting.

RIGHT: *You can't get much fancier than this! At first glance, it may seem like one, big array of 'stuff', but if you look more closely, you will realise that it is, in fact, very carefully considered – which is why it isn't overwhelming. I have laid strips of silk velvet on top of the cloth – an old French sheet dyed chartreuse – and used them to define and accommodate each place setting. Wine and water are placed in the spaces between the strips, and the candlesticks are arranged symmetrically. You see what I mean – everything is highly organised. I rarely have a table without at least one set of coloured glasses, and here there are two sets. The combination of amethyst and cranberry is about as good as it gets.*

BELOW: *Flowers cut short and clustered in glasses – these are Georgian rummers – have the prettiness of old-fashioned posies.*

BELOW RIGHT: *I find this service, by Meissen, particularly pleasing. The flowers seem to have fallen rather carelessly over the surface, which is utterly charming.*

RIGHT: *Crystal is a glorious medium for enhancing the sparkle of candlelight. It also picks up surrounding colours in a subtle way – as here, where it further enriches the warm colour scheme of the tabletop. The candlesticks with classically inspired columns are from my Collection and make marvellous punctuation amidst the antique crystal.*

# PICNICS

The part of my house that was originally the schoolmistress's cottage looks across a ha-ha to what was once a farmed field but is now a wild-flower meadow. It's the perfect spot for a picnic, even though it's only yards from my front door. I always have a couple of folding tables for setting out the food, and canvas-slung, directors' chairs for those who prefer to sit rather than spread out on cushions on the grass. I don't see why a picnic shouldn't be, in its own way, every bit as stylish as a meal in a more permanent location, so I take along full-length tablecloths and masses of fabric to lay on the ground, in lots of different colours, to create an inviting vignette. Hopefully, the sun will shine, so umbrellas are important – and if it rains, they are essential! I always prefer to buy organic food if I can, and it seems especially appropriate in the close-to-nature setting of a picnic.

There is a certain holiday mood about a picnic, so it's an opportunity to enjoy the sort of rustic, souvenir plates and dishes that have great charm but are not always easy to use in other contexts. Something else that often appears on our picnics is my retro radio – but only played very quietly, of course!

*LEFT: Having a picnic in our wild-flower meadow is one of the joys of summer. It's all very relaxed, with lots of cushions to lounge on – these ones are big and square, rather like French pillows. The covers are made of linen, in wonderful colours that have an oriental depth to them. When you look at the house from here, you can see how the space between the original schoolmistress's cottage (at left) and the schoolhouse (at right) has been roofed over to join the two buildings and create a new entrance and hall.*

*TOP RIGHT: I was given these handpainted plates by my friend Adam; they record restaurants in Italy.*

*CENTRE RIGHT: Cheese, tomatoes, chicory… nothing too elaborate but all delectable when eaten outside.*

*RIGHT: I have a number of folding tables, chairs and umbrellas for picnics. They're very practical, not just for carrying out to the meadow but also for taking in the car if we're driving into the countryside. It's a bit of squeeze to get them all in my Fiat Cinquecento – but we manage.*

LEFT: *Willie goes organic! When I take sandwiches to a picnic, I wrap them in greaseproof paper and denote the filling by the colour of the twine, then I top them off with a flower, which looks pretty and chimes with the idea of organic food.*

RIGHT: *If you are going to decorate your picnic tables with cut flowers, be careful what you choose. Don't use anything that looks as though you have bought it at a florists, and avoid fancy containers. Here, the daisies and cornflowers have been picked from the meadow where we are having our picnic and placed, rather randomly, in coloured-glass jars.*

BELOW: *Tumblers are more stable than stem glasses for picnics and look more informal. The smell of fresh mint really does evoke the season and its colour is fabulous in conjunction with amethyst.*

GARDEN LIVING

LEFT: *This is where I sit outside if the weather looks unpredictable. If it starts to pour, I can dash back into the garden room – and have a little snooze. On fine days, it's a suntrap in the late afternoon, a perfect time and place for a glass of wine.*

RIGHT: *The garden room glimpsed through a small gothic window. Adding a window in this style made sense with the architecture of the house.*

PREVIOUS PAGES: *The different colours, textures and sizes of the leaves create a layered effect as you look beyond this old stone wall to the flower garden. The wall is terminated with a circular 'pillar', which is topped with a sphere.*

# THE GARDEN ROOM

Everyone who leads a busy life appreciates somewhere quiet to escape to, and this is my bolthole: a small stone building, close to the house but detached from it. It was previously an ugly, tumbledown shack, which didn't serve any useful purpose, so we rebuilt it and transformed it into a sitting room in miniature, where one can be on one's own. ('Two's company', they say – but sometimes one can be fun!) I use the room mainly as a place to read or think about new design projects (or even write books!), happy in the knowledge that – and this is very deliberate – there is neither telephone nor computer to disturb the peaceful atmosphere. With French doors leading directly into the garden, it's a light, airy space, which is hung with numerous paintings, none of any great importance but all with something that makes them special to me.

LEFT: *There's not a huge amount of space in the garden room – but enough for a few of us to have summery drinks in shelter. Blackberry, strawberry… what glorious colours these fruits produce. No wonder the little mouse is taking such an interest in them!*

RIGHT: *Immediately outside the garden room is a gravelled area with a folding table and a stone 'tree trunk' on which I stand plants or sometimes sit if I haven't got round to bringing out a chair. Beyond, you can see one of the garden's obelisks. Some openwork obelisks look too flimsy for my taste – but not this one. Its sturdy construction makes an attractive architectural feature even when it isn't acting as a climbing frame. It came from the terrace of the late, wonderful garden guru, Rosemary Verey, who lived nearby.*

PREVIOUS PAGES: *The garden room is furnished with an eclectic mix: Edwardian-style wicker chairs, a linen-union-covered armchair, a circular oak table and a brightly coloured hexagonal table I bought while on a trip to India. The old Turkish carpet has found its final resting place here. It had previously been in the house but became so tatty that I had to replace it. However, I didn't throw it away, as the great thing about an old rug is that you can always cut off the threadbare bits and downsize it for another place.*

# LUNCH OUTDOORS

I seize every opportunity I can to have lunch outside. Somehow, the fresh air sharpens one's tastebuds and food tastes especially delicious. One part of my garden is arranged specifically for dining, with a wooden table and benches that have weathered over the years and now have a wonderful patina of age. The table is a straightforward, traditional design with a slatted top, while the benches and chairs are more decorative, with curving top rails and a slightly Chinese motif used for the backs. The furniture looks good all year round – an important consideration in winter – and is robust enough to be left outdoors, whatever the weather. It stands on old stone slabs, which provide a firm surface and dry off quickly after rain, and is sheltered by a dry-stone wall. Against the wall, a table with a stone top and curvilinear iron base forms a platform for plants in flowerpots and a stone urn. I never think that the table-setting for a casual lunch outdoors should be taken too seriously but it certainly shouldn't be thrown together without any thought – that would be a let-down and diminish the enjoyment. All you have to do is choose some cheerful accessories and stick to a colour scheme, which need not be overly subtle. Here is a really good example of when a fabric runner is better than a cloth, as it allows the table's attractive texture to be seen.

LEFT: *I always put cushions on wooden garden furniture – after all, you do need a bit of comfort – but they are not covered in anything fragile. Here, their covers are made of good scraps of heavy linen salvaged from damaged tablecloths – the sort you pick up in village flea markets all over Europe. No matter how many flowers there are around about, I still like to have some on the table. Sprays of* Alchemilla mollis *look good in a white jar with blue bands echoing the stripes on the cushions.*

ABOVE RIGHT: *Checks, spots and stripes: these classic motifs live happily together. Nothing could be simpler than this fold for a napkin. It's instant but decorative, and I sometimes hide a little trinket inside.*

RIGHT: *This is all about 'red'. In another context, I sometimes use these tall glasses as vases placed down the middle of the table; my friend Nicola, who has similar glasses, puts tea-lights in them in the evening.*

ABOVE: *A vintage tablecloth with irrelevant cocktail recipes can be amusing used in this casual way.*

LEFT: *Serving a country-style rosé is made more special by decanting it into a simple glass carafe.*

RIGHT: *With their clusters of white 'pinheads', the flower heads of this form of cow parsley have a tapestry-like quality. Plants with white flowers and vibrant-green foliage are some of the most useful for arrangements, as they give a 'lift'.*

PREVIOUS PAGES: *Many successful gardens are divided into 'rooms'. This is my outdoor dining room, enclosed by low, green walls. Seen at right is an old fruit-picker's ladder.*

# THE SUMMERHOUSE

Sometimes the simplest things give the most pleasure – and this little summerhouse, with its weathered boarding and humble balustrade, is a case in point. As soon as spring arrives, I'm out there, sweeping away the leaves and getting it ready for those warm, summer afternoons when it's one of our most treasured places for tea. It's very small, with space for three or four friends at most, and it's rustic, so the whole occasion is inevitably informal – even laying the cloth at an angle suits the carefree mood.

ABOVE: *The nostalgic associations of summerhouses often inspire the things I choose for the table. The shiny teapot, for example, has a pleasingly evocative character.*

LEFT: *One of the best things about our summerhouse is that it's set on a revolving base, so we can turn it to face the sun or, if that's too dazzling, swivel it in the other direction.*

RIGHT: *When I pick flowers for the summerhouse, I don't want them to look stiff and contrived. I mix varieties and colours, and I bunch them loosely in casual containers – china pots from the pantry, or jars standing in baskets, as in the picture at left. A glass dome protects food from persistent insects without hiding from view the goodies beneath.*

RIGHT: *'Life's a bowl of cherries': how tempting they look piled up in a stemmed glass bowl. The old cups and saucers don't match the plates, but it simply doesn't matter – they look pretty, as do the rose petals scattered round the polenta cake. Leaning up in the corner are some croquet mallets – we'll have another game after tea!*

BELOW LEFT: *Too good to refuse: home-baked polenta cake and traditional English iced buns.*

BELOW RIGHT: *Even in the height of summer, it can be chilly, so I usually provide some lightweight wraps. This one, hanging behind the slatted chair, has an embroidered border.*

The summerhouse is adjacent to the lawn where we play croquet, a game we love and that has given us many hours of pleasure – even if some of us have been known to resort to unworthy tactics! Tea is all part of the ritual, and so is setting up the table. This kind of situation calls for pattern, such as you see in the picture below. The medley of designs characterising the check tablecloth, bordered wrap and pretty ceramics is harmonised by a shared palette of blue and white – a combination that is hard to beat in any location and at any time of year, but in a garden, and in summer, it never fails to please.

LEFT: *Inside the summerhouse, behind the basket of flowers, are some of our venerable wooden croquet mallets and iron hoops. Pretty baskets are invariably a temptation for me – this one is high-sided enough to conceal the glass containers holding the flowers.*

BELOW LEFT: *If I run out of space for flowers on the table, I use a hanging 'posy pot' in the shape of a half-round barrel and fix it to the wall. One of the benefits of rustic, wooden walls is that you don't have to be fussy about making holes in them.*

BELOW: *When we are playing croquet, I put out a few folding chairs, in case anyone wants to take a break and watch the others do battle.*

## THE VEGETABLE GARDEN

A short distance away is the vegetable garden, which is partially enclosed by a dry-stone wall and has some fine old trees as a backdrop. Essentially, this is a functional place, intended primarily for growing edible plants, but there is something so special about it that it's all too easy to spend many hours here, just sitting and pondering rather than getting down to work. The greenhouse is a simple affair, with a brick base supporting timber-framed glazing above, and is home to a number of plants all year round while having enough space for propagating and, if necessary, over-wintering some tender species.

LEFT: *The greenhouse is at one end of the garden and is surrounded mainly by grass, but there is an area of paving to the right, which is useful for leaning stakes against the stone wall and setting down watering cans and tools.*

LEFT: *There are grass paths between the vegetable beds as they make access easier for weeding and harvesting. Netting is all too essential for outwitting the birds as they will literally peck the place clean if they are given half a chance. Flowerpots keep the netting in place and ensure that the ends of the sticks can't give you a nasty jab.*

BELOW: *Bamboo sticks tied together are a simple means of constructing a framework to support fruit and vegetables.*

RIGHT: *The stone from the local quarries is one of the loveliest characteristics of the Cotswolds. It is used for the grandest churches as well as for vernacular cottages and outbuildings, such as this, which adjoins the vegetable garden. The door is pure Beatrix Potter — it brings to mind Mr. McGregor's garden.*

BELOW: *Next to the stripling tomato plant are some wicker cloches that look like quirky hats. These are used to cover the rhubarb before the real forcers are put on.*

# THE FLOWER GARDEN

When I go to our house in the country, one of the first things I do is walk round the garden. Like all gardens, it can change so quickly that I only have to be away for a day or two for it to take on a totally different appearance – and there's a real excitement in that. I don't claim to be very knowledgeable about gardening but I find it rewarding and relaxing, a great way to unwind after working during the week in a city or after long hours of travelling for business. My favourite kinds of gardens, especially in the country, are those with old-fashioned, 'cottagey' flowers. I love their colours and scents. Above all, though, I think a garden should be sympathetic to its location and the house it adjoins. My house isn't grand, so I don't want anything too pretentious outside. I do, however, like some structure – some symmetrical paths and vistas to 'frame' the planting.

RIGHT: *Gravel offsets terracotta pots and beds with old-fashioned plants, including the stately foxglove.*

BELOW: *Roses are some of my all-time favourite flowers, and I especially love those with a beautiful scent. This pale and delicious rose is unbelievably heady and musky.*

BELOW: *Astrantia is another good choice in a country garden. It has a rather cheerful look and goes well with other pink- and mauve-flowering plants. There are many varieties of astrantia, all of which behave differently.*

BELOW: *The flowers I tend to favour are pink, blue and mauve. This iris, growing alongside the decorative feverfew, is typical. The texture of the petals looks lovely even in the rain.*

LEFT: *The garden room is seen here across the flower garden. Aquilegia, or Granny's Bonnet as it is often called, gives delicate height in the foreground, while the foxglove at right makes a bolder statement. Gates and fences in natural wood can look very harmonious in a country setting, but in some situations I like the freshness of white paint – here, the painted fence provides a punctuation mark.*

BELOW LEFT: *There's no escaping my passion for peonies! They start out as unpromising, tight balls and end up like this – beautifully blowsy. This one is a striking, crimson pink.*

BELOW: *Scabious… for me, no country garden would be complete without this pleasing perennial, with its flowers borne atop long stems. I often grow it in large pots, which is not all that usual.*

# FLOWERS FOR THE HOUSE

Most of the plants in my garden have the sort of flowers that I enjoy seeing in the house. The dilemma is that I don't want to cut so many of them for indoors that I leave the plants outside looking bare – though it always astonishes me how quickly new blooms appear. In fact, many plants are positively encouraged by the wielding of secateurs. When I'm going round the garden on a cutting mission, I carry with me whatever containers come to hand – and I often think that flowers look particularly ravishing when they are put wantonly in these basic things.

LEFT: *Blue catmint always looks well when mixed with white and pink flowers, sharpened by the lime-green tones of alchemilla.*

RIGHT: *Wicker is such a lovely foil for flowers that when I've finished my cutting, I sometimes put the basket down just so that I can stand back and feast my eyes on the combination. The texture of the old, stone wall is a perfect complement.*

BELOW: *These peonies come from my own garden, but if I need more, I buy some at the market and intermix them.*

LEFT: *With the exquisite colours of the flowers and leaves playing off each other, and the background of mellow Cotswold stone and an old wooden bench, this picture encapsulates everything I hold dear about my garden in the country.*

RIGHT: *Here are the same flowers brought indoors and sorted into two different groups. The flowers I have chosen for the jug at left — mainly peonies, Alchemilla mollis and salvia — have a comparatively vibrant look that marries well with the solidity of the white earthenware. Old jugs, such as this, with moulded relief, make excellent vessels for flowers, especially if the arrangements are kept informal. In contrast, the tall, flaring shape and lightness of the clear-glass vase at right are good foils for taller, more delicately coloured flowers. The new, silvery growth from a weeping pear forms the backbone of this arrangement. When I prune, I always keep in mind that the 'woody' snippings can be useful in this way.*

# GARDEN BENCHES

My garden, which runs round three sides of the house, is laid out as a series of 'rooms' but with no hard divisions between them to halt the flow. Each room has its own character, and all the rooms are furnished with benches. I consider benches – which come in so many different styles – not only as aesthetic features but also as invitations to sit on those days when idleness gets the better of me. I once came across a quote that went something along the lines of: 'Exercise? Yes, I adore it. There's nothing I like better than a good, brisk sit.' I don't know who said it, but it must have been someone after my own heart!

LEFT: *The flower garden, where the plants are rather cottagey, has a traditional, unassuming, timber bench with slatted seat and back. This sort of hard-wood bench takes on a beautiful, silvery colour as it ages.*

RIGHT: *A metal bench looks more in keeping in this setting, which has an architectural backdrop. Rather than let the bench 'float' in the space, I have contained it visually with pots raised on plinths.*

LEFT: *I must own more cushions than anyone I know. I think the green-and-white fabric seen here suits the soft tones of the weathered timber bench and surrounding planting.*

RIGHT: *When autumn comes, and you begin to see russet tones appearing and feel a chill in the air, you appreciate having a throw to hand, such as this paisley one in colours that pick up the seasonal ambience and the colour of the terracotta pots. I often spread a travel-rug on the seat of the bench, which looks (and feels) cosseting.*

PREVIOUS PAGES: *This bench is by far the most unconventional in my garden — and, to me, it's the best. What an amazing shape! It's made of concrete, about 8 feet long, and probably dates from the 1930s. For the extraordinary lines to be appreciated fully, the bench needed something fairly solid behind it but of a totally different texture, so I planted a hedge of copper beech. The curves of the bench make such a bold statement that no curlicue-patterned fabric could compete with them — that's my reason for covering the cushions with a simple, graphic stripe. Note the pompoms, which are tiny references to the hefty balls on the ground.*

CITY LIVING

# THE HALL

The hall in my city apartment is miles apart from the hall in my house in the country – and I don't just mean geographically. For one thing, it's smaller, but the real difference is in the colours. Here, in town, the look is darker and more dramatic, with the walls painted in a robust shade of chestnut, which is offset by white woodwork. Halls are very much 'first impression' spaces, so you need to think carefully about what sort of effect you are after – and stick to it. If you want something strong, as I did here, it's no good cluttering the place up with bits and pieces, so I have used only two pieces of furniture, both with good shapes, and two large, arresting pictures, plus a natural sculpture. I say 'natural' because it is, in fact, a single piece of petrified ebony. As the subjects of the pictures have 'woody' associations, and the base of the table looks like twisted branches, there is a strong theme going on here.

LEFT: *In this view from the dining room to the hall, you can see an x-frame oak stool from the Arts and Crafts period and a picture of a wood-gatherer, probably painted around 1870, which I bought in France.*

RIGHT: *The table is mid-nineteenth-century Scandinavian with a later, hand-hewn limestone top. Above the natural sculpture of petrified ebony is 'The Woodcutter', a painting by Somerset artist John Caple.*

PREVIOUS PAGES: *Our apartment is in a mansion block, built in 1900, overlooking a London park and still with its original iron balcony.*

# THE DRAWING ROOM

This room has a smart, rather architectural feel, due to some extent to the graphic form of the new chimneypieces at each end of the room. Plentiful, natural light comes through the two tall windows and the shorter windows in the bay. The different heights of the windows determined different treatments – curtains for the tall openings and roman blinds for the lower ones – but all in the same silk jacquard. The rich macchiato shade used for the walls is a strong foil for the lime greens and terracottas that predominate in most of the soft furnishings.

FAR LEFT: *The contemporary pots by Ursula Morley Price, on the table between the pair of armchairs, have fins of unbelievable fineness.*

ABOVE LEFT: *The mid-twentieth-century Danish lamp, with its spiral base, is a great favourite of mine. The car, bought in Morocco, is less of a 'design' piece but relaxes the composition.*

BELOW LEFT: *Using two different fabrics is livelier than sticking to one fabric. Here, natural linen is partnered with cut velvet.*

RIGHT: *An early-twentieth-century architect's table, bought in Provence, has been reinvented for today and for another purpose: I have taken the general form as my inspiration and lowered it for use in a drawing room. The original table came from gifted decorator Dick Dumas.*

PREVIOUS PAGES: *Typically in a room of this period, the chimney-breast breaks forward, creating recesses to either side that lend themselves perfectly to shelves. Built-in 'units' – the sort with cupboards in the lower half – could look too traditional (and predictable!) if you are aiming for an up-to-date feel: chunky, timber shelves, pure and simple, are better. Above the chimney-piece is a painting of a woman, by Fred Yates, from 1965.*

LEFT: *Above the chimneypiece at the bay end of the room is another painting by Fred Yates, this one executed some 35 years later than 'Bessie in the Blue Hat'. Fancifully, I sometimes think the expressions on the faces of the characters are a reaction to the room's mix of furniture, which includes an Egyptian-revival stool, made by Liberty in the 1920s, a pair of 1840s fruitwood armchairs and a mid-twentieth-century, Danish rosewood chair.*

BELOW: *The French bergères are upholstered in three fabrics, including one in kantha work, an Indian technique of stitching in patterns, often in straight lines.*

RIGHT: *The chestnut-wood table that sits in the bay is from the William Yeoward Collection and has a top with 32 sections of veneer on a base made of solid-wood. It's a stunning piece of work.*

BELOW: *I have always been drawn to the vases made by Fulham Pottery in the mid twentieth century, which were inspired by the forms of classical urns, but they have become very collectable lately. The shapes are excellent for flowers, especially if the stems are cut short, and the satin glaze is a gentle complement.*

RIGHT: *The five-branch, crystal candelabrum on the circular, chestnut table is from my Collection and is a major Yeoward statement. You can't miss it when you come into the room! The 'tree' lamps on the 1940s, Continental side-table are ormolu, and between them hangs a painting by Alberto Morrocco.*

# THE DINING ROOM

The dining room is the apartment's central axis, with five doors of different sizes leading off it, plus a window awkwardly placed in one corner. So many openings gave the space a rather disjointed appearance, and it was obvious that something was needed to pull the whole thing together, so we lined the entire perimeter – walls and doors alike – with plain, painted panelling, as a form of disguise. In our re-arrangement of the layout of the apartment, the drawing room leads off the dining room and I felt it was important to give significance to this entrance by introducing full-height, double doors here. There is another advantage: when the doors are open during the day, masses of borrowed, natural light comes through to the dining room from the drawing room.

RIGHT: *Looking through the new, full-height, double doors to the drawing room.*

BELOW: *The dining room is like an inner hall. Consequently, when we are not entertaining, I keep it simple, with nothing on the table except the contemporary leaf sculpture by Hervé Van der Straeten.*

In the daytime, the dining table is left virtually bare and there are usually only four chairs round it, but when we have guests for dinner, we bring in more chairs – the table seats eight comfortably – and dress up the table with a generously long cloth and, of course, beautiful china and crystal. I love colour on a table but the restraint of 'no colour' can also be extremely effective, especially in the sophisticated ambience of a city. If you opt for a monochrome setting with clear crystal, the way to instil interest is to choose glasses in various shapes, with and without cutting and etching. Remember, too, that containers can lead double lives: here, a Champagne cooler with horizontal cutting makes a glorious vase for roses while, on a much smaller scale, salt cellars are ideal for miniature cacti.

PREVIOUS PAGES: *The chairs follow my rule for dining rooms: they must look as interesting from behind as from in front, as they will be seen from both angles. Conversely, I didn't want to draw attention to the awkwardly placed window, squashed into the corner, so I have played it down – no curtains and nothing on the sill. I prefer the attention to be focused on the paintings, both by John Brown, to either side of the window.*

LEFT: *Apart from the plant leaves, the only colour on the table is in the muted tones of the hand-embroidered, linen placemats and of the hand-block-printed napkins.*

RIGHT: *A Champagne cooler holds massed roses; salt cellars contain a single cactus.*

We have a lot of friends who enjoy card-playing evenings. On those occasions, we remove the dining table and replace it with two smaller tables, one (with a baize top) for cards and the other for supper. Both tables are my designs and are made of American walnut with nickel inlay. The bookcase, which is made of chestnut wood – this, incidentally, has wonderful figuring – adds a library connotation to the dining room, which prevents the space from looking too obviously like a room used solely for eating, and it helps, visually and atmospherically, in its transformation for card-playing.

BELOW: *The twinned tables have pyramidal bases. To the left of the bookcase, you can see two of the room's five doors, disguised to meld in with the walls by the continuous use of painted panelling.*

RIGHT: *This is the card table, with a baize top framed with nickel and walnut. Inside is a veritable compendium of different games.*

BELOW RIGHT: *A glass of 'something' is encouraging when you are playing cards – especially if you are losing! I like cocktails and they are a good reason to bring out glasses of different shapes.*

For our card-playing evenings, the food is informal and doesn't require too much last-minute preparation. Soup, for instance, served with crusty bread, is a good beginning, but whatever I cook, I make sure the presentation on the table is a pleasure to look at, with beautiful glasses and well designed, if unpretentious, china. White ranunculas in a big, early-Regency goblet fuse the line between elegance and informality.

# THE KITCHEN

If you like cooking, the chances are that you spend a lot of time in the kitchen, so it has to be a pleasant room to be in. This is our kitchen and, as you can see, it has a very cheerful aspect, with a small table where Colin and I tend to eat when we are alone or perhaps have just two friends to supper. One of the things I like most about the room is the floor, which is laid with linoleum hand-cut to a design taken from a 1930s headscarf. The pattern is very bold but the geometry is controlled, with a series of circles contained within a regular grid, so the overall effect isn't disturbing. There is only one significant piece of 'art' in the room – a poster advertising the premiere in Milan of *Some Like it Hot*. From the point of view of cooking, there is everything we need to rustle up an enjoyable meal, but the room doesn't – thank goodness – have the air of a hard-edged 'professional' kitchen with acres of stainless steel.

LEFT: *Around the mid-twentieth-century Danish table are chairs upholstered in one of my herringbone weaves, 'Barancona'. I designed the chairs very specifically for rooms where space is limited: the trick is small scale, big comfort.*

TOP RIGHT: *The table is set with wooden plates, the surface of which has been covered with fragments of dyed eggshell, then lacquered. They were made in Vietnam, a long way from the source of the glasses by Venetian designer Carlo Moretti.*

RIGHT: *Contrasting forms of cactus: hand-painted on plates bought on the west coast of America, and real in crystal salt cellars.*

On the narrow strip of wall between the two windows is a papier-mâché head of a giraffe. How can you not feel cheered when you come into a room and are greeted by a friendly face such as this? I have a real passion for papier mâché, which is a terrific medium for creating all kinds of objects. On the worktop are yet more cacti. I love these plants for their quirky, sculptural shapes and consider them much under-used in interior decoration.

## MY BEDROOM AND BATHROOM

The thinking behind the look of this room refers back to those glorious suites of bedroom furniture that were very much 'the thing' in the 1930s. I designed the bed and flanking chests of drawers as a unified group, made of chestnut wood with bands of nickel. These materials have visual qualities that set them apart from other woods and metals – the timber is wonderfully rich in tone and grain, while the metal is less harsh-looking than, say, steel or chrome – and, together, they make a fine marriage. I have also used chestnut for the panelled wall behind the bed. I had the timber cut into panels because I wanted to create the illusion of a flush surface right across the width of the room while, in fact, the panels to either side of the bed are doors (with hidden latches) that conceal cupboards. The rather masculine materials and shapes of the furniture are softened by the textiles, particularly the linen which, flocked, lines the room's unpanelled walls and, unflocked, is gathered into a sunburst on the underside of the bed canopy. The hand-appliquéed cushions were made to my designs by the talented Yama.

LEFT: *The chestnut four-poster integrates with the panelled wall behind.*

BELOW LEFT: *The stool at the end of the bed is perfect for two purposes: first, for placing the bedcover when not in use, and, secondly, as a stair for Poppy, our Jack Russell terrier.*

BELOW: *On the chests of drawers to either side of the bed are tumblers and lamps from my Collections. The technique for making the lamp bases was heavily inspired by Ancient Roman glass and involves drizzling a thread of molten crystal over the body of the vessel.*

In contrast to the
chestnut panelling, the
rest of the room is lined
with my 'Hortense'
flocked linen, which has
been paper-backed to
make it suitable for use
on walls. I find this is a
thoroughly worthwhile
decoration device, as
fabric on the walls
undoubtedly gives 'depth'
to a room. The curtains
are made of the same
fabric. An important
consideration for me was
to have a bedcover
made of a washable
fabric, as our much-loved
Jack Russell often sneaks
into the room. You can
see her charming portrait
on the chest-of-drawers.

LEFT: *This view points up the difference in decoration in the bedroom and bathroom: I like the concept of each individual space being given its own character by changes in texture and palette but nevertheless having an overall harmony. In the bedroom, there is a sense of luxe derived from the soft appearance of the textiles, in particular the flocked linen that is used on three of the walls and for the curtains and pelmet (which, incidentally, have been given an extra dimension with edging bands of contrasting silk velvet). In the bathroom, the look is much more graphic, with plain surfaces and painted shutters.*

The 'sleeping quarters' are at the opposite end of the apartment from the drawing room and kitchen, and are self-contained behind a door leading off the dining room. The idea was to give the feeling of being in a very expensive hotel suite, where bedroom, bathroom and dressing areas all blend together in a single entity. The bedroom and bathroom are separated by wide, sliding doors made of opaque glass, which gives privacy but retains a feeling of space. Unlike in the bedroom, the walls in the bathroom are painted, and the windows have shutters rather than curtains. Apart from being more practical in an essentially functional room, shutters are a good solution if you have windows of different sizes and with different sill heights, especially in a small space. The graphic nature of shutters has a unifying effect, whereas curtains or blinds would draw attention to the irregularities and also make the room seem smaller.

LEFT: *The bath is set into a surround of chestnut wood, echoing the timber seen in the bedroom. The taps and water spout are built into the wall, thus keeping the lines of the bath uninterrupted. The wall-hung towel-rail frees up space lower down in the room and has a linear affinity with the slatted shutters.*

RIGHT: *The sliding doors between the bedroom and bathroom have panes of opaque glass within a timber framework. At this end of the bathroom are a generously wide basin and the room's only piece of furniture – a mid-century Danish armchair. By now you will have gathered that this style of furniture is one of my all-time favourites. I admire it not only for the superb timbers used but also for the quality of the craftsmanship.*

# MY DRESSING ROOM

Our apartment has two dressing rooms: Colin's, which opens directly off the bedroom, and mine, which is hardly more than a step away from the bedroom and is large enough to accommodate a bed – useful if I want a quick nap before going out or for the occasional overnight guest. The bed is designed to be pulled out into the room, so you don't have to sleep right up against the wall, and there is space beneath it for storing shoes. The walls at either end of the bed are canted, leaving triangular spaces which I have used for low, built-in cupboards. Virtually all the drawings in the room are of theatrical subjects and most of them are propped up on narrow shelves rather than hung directly on the walls, which is a good way to display pictures of different shapes and sizes, as it creates a neat 'line-up' and looks interesting. Adjoining the dressing room is my lovely power-shower room.

LEFT: *The walls are faced with fabric that has been paper-backed for hanging. The theatrical drawings are by, amongst others, Oliver Messel, Christian Bérard and John MacFarlane.*

RIGHT: *Perched on a shellwork tray by the bed is an Art Deco toucan jug. What a great character! The glass is 'cased' crystal, made by a method that involves putting a layer of colour over clear crystal; when the coloured surface is cut, the clear crystal is exposed.*

TOP LEFT: *The shower room that opens off the dressing room is reflected here in an overscaled, nickel-framed 'fob-watch' mirror from the William Yeoward Collection, which is a metre in diameter. Also reflected in the mirror are the chestnut doors of the wardrobe in the dressing room.*

LEFT: *Colourful cotton hand-towels, which we collect on our travels, hang above the basin in the shower room. The rosary, comprising rough ceramic beads, was made by French designer Jacqueline Morabito.*

RIGHT: *The woodcut by Hugo Guinness depicts a Jack Russell terrier just like our Poppy, who plays such a prominent part in our lives. The other animal here is a blackbird, stylized into a lamp, dating from the 1950s. The fabrics are a mixture of vintage – the quilted ones – and new pieces, the latter from the William Yeoward Collection.*

ELEGY REFLECTIONS ON ANGKOR JOHN MCDERMOTT

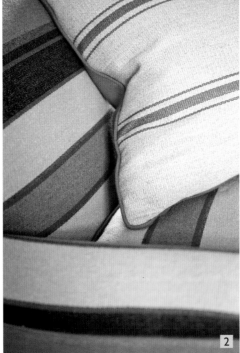

# ICONIC YEOWARD

When I look back over twenty-five years of my work, there are certain themes that seem to recur: form, texture, colour, quality and, above all, what I term 'practical glamour'. When you buy something for your home, it is essential that the piece will give you continued pleasure, not just immediate gratification followed by years of disappointment.

The images on these pages include some of my favourite pieces from the various Yeoward Collections of crystal and glass, furniture, fabrics, lighting, china and accessories, and in particular remind me of the pleasure that I have taken in working with my colleagues to produce these fine results.

**7**

**8**

**9**

**1** *The pleasing combination of walnut and nickel on my card table.*
**2** *Textures, colours and stripes – all bound together in these delicious fabrics.*
**3** *Some pieces from our Collection of decorative crystal centrepieces, inspired by mid-nineteenth-century examples, mixed here with eighteenth-century pieces from my personal archive.*
**4** *The bookcase designed for our drawing room in the country. It was beautifully proportioned by John Vince and elegantly painted in 'many shades of bone' by the lovely Alice Clark.*
**5** *A drizzled crystal studio vase in perfect sky-blue.*
**6** *Our 'Flavia' goblet, sublimely interpreted by Tim Jenkins, derived from an original made around 1790.*
**7** *The perfect striped cushion.*
**8** *A marvellous high-ball tumbler inspired by a nineteenth-century American design and based on woven wicker-clad glass containers for wines and spirits.*
**9** *Hand-appliquéd panels designed individually for upholstery.*
**10** *My chestnut and nickel four-poster bed with matching chests.*

**10**

# INDEX

# AUTHOR'S ACKNOWLEDGEMENTS

Gavin Kingcome, who worked tirelessly on this book and photographed exquisitely the very essence of both country and city life, must be thanked for his truly exceptional patience and constant encouragement and enthusiasm.

Leonie Highton made the writing of the book a real joy and must be thanked, too, for all her care and kindness.

So many talented and truly gifted people have I come across in my work who have helped, designed, commented and made things that I live with day to day that I wanted to thank at least a few:

Samantha Kingcome, Tim and Dana Jenkins, Tricia Guild, Chris Halsey, Paul Bramfitt, Joe Trinanes, Jane and Jonathan Fyson.

Toby Lorford, Nicholas Carter, Susan Crewe, Leslie Ferguson, Philip Adler, Libbs Lewis, Hoggy Nicholls, Rupert Thomas, Christopher Clark, Nina Campbell, Sally Powell, Tony Palmer, Gary Cooper, Jonathan Davies, Michael Nicholson, Giles Kime, Lisa Gibson-Keynes, Sandie Howard, Christopher Masson, Andrew Long, Mark Smith, Danny Parnes, Deborah Barker, Darren Shick, Christine Wood, Yama Maskara, Stephen Woodhams, Sarah King, Anita Patel, Michael Williamson, Alexa Stephenson, Gillian Haslam, Carol Paul, Fay Cariaso, Jenny South, Kevin Nicholls, Richard Dineen, Helen Lewis, Philippa Gibson, Erich Salatin, Andrew Christie, Chris Smith, Polly Lister, Brian Freidman, Su Daybell, Paul Emrys-Roberts, John Martin, Colin Hawkins, Roger Hall, Joseph.

And last but not least, Cindy Richards for her continued vision and support and for allowing me the freedom to make another beautiful book.

*For further information on William Yeoward, visit:*

FURNITURE, FABRICS, LIGHTING,
ACCESSORIES, INTERIORS
www.williamyeoward.com

WILLIAM YEOWARD CRYSTAL,
BONE CHINA, COUNTRY GLASS
www.williamyeowardcrystal.com

WILLIAM YEOWARD FURNITURE IN
THE UNITED STATES
www.yeowardfurnitureusa.com